Suddenly Rich

Story by Carmel Reilly

Illustrations by Victoria Layne

Suddenly Rich

Text: Carmel Reilly
Publishers: Tania Mazzeo and Eliza Webb
Series consultant: Amanda Sutera
Hands on Heads Consulting
Editor: Kate Daniel
Project editor: Annabel Smith
Designer: Jess Kelly
Project designer: Danielle Maccarone
Illustrations: Victoria Layne
Production controller: Renee Tome

NovaStar

ISBN 978 0 17 033505 8

Cengage Learning Australia
Level 5, 80 Dorcas Street
Southbank VIC 3006 Australia
Phone: 1300 790 853
Email: aust.nelsonprimary@cengage.com

For learning solutions, visit **cengage.com.au**

Printed in China by 1010 Printing International Ltd
1 2 3 4 5 6 7 29 28 27 26 25

Nelson acknowledges the Traditional Owners and Custodians of the lands of all First Nations Peoples. We pay respect to Elders past and present, and extend that respect to all First Nations Peoples today.

Contents

Chapter 1

A Big Win

I knew something was up straightaway when Mum woke me early one Sunday morning. It was the beginning of the summer holidays. No school, and no weekend sports. I was enjoying a sleep-in.

"Willow," Mum said, nudging me.

"What's going on?" I squealed, slightly alarmed. Did we have to go somewhere? Was the house on fire?

"Oh, it's nothing terrible, darling," said Mum brightly. "In fact, Dad and I have some very good news for you all."

"You do?" I mumbled. I glanced across the room to Freya, my older sister. But her bed was empty, which was very odd. When did Freya ever get up before me?

Dad and Freya were already in the kitchen when I sleepily walked in. Mum was waking up our little brother, Zeb. He'd been asleep on his foldaway bed in the living room. We only had a tiny two-bedroom house and, since he turned seven last year, Zeb had refused to share a room with us, his sisters.

Finally, Mum and Zeb sat down at the crowded kitchen table.

Mum looked nervous, and I started to feel nervous too.

"You know how Dad and I sometimes buy lottery tickets?" she said at last. "Well, yesterday we won first prize!"

"We did?" said Freya.

"No way!" I blurted.

"But what does that mean?" asked Freya.

"It means we're going to be really rich, doesn't it?" piped up Zeb.

Mum laughed. “It does! It will change everything for us.”

“We’ll finally be able to buy a home of our own,” said Dad.

“Imagine!” cried Freya. “My own bedroom!”

“What about a new car?” I asked, thinking how good it would be not to have to drive around in our embarrassing old wreck.

Mum grinned. “I was thinking of one of those luxury cars they advertise on TV.”

“Or a stretch limo,” added Zeb enthusiastically.

I felt like pinching myself. How amazing to wake up and find out you’re suddenly rich!

I couldn’t wait to tell my best friend, Laney.

After breakfast, I raced around to Laney's place. She lived in a small apartment with her mum, not far from our house. She and I had been friends since I moved schools in grade three.

"Laney, you'll never guess what!" I yelled, as she opened the door to me. "We won the lottery! My family is rich!"

Laney laughed as though she didn't believe me. She and I joked around a lot. I could see she thought I was just being silly.

"You know all those things we've wanted to do, like learn surfing or go to the adventure park or those interactive exhibitions?" I said. "We can do them now."

"Really?' she said.

"Yes, starting tomorrow. Do you want to go to the aquarium?"

"Okay," she agreed, with an uncertain laugh.

"And we'll pay," I added.

The next day, after exploring the aquarium, Dad took us to a café for lunch.

"I'm not hungry," said Laney politely, when Dad asked her what she wanted to eat.

"It's on us!" said Dad.

"We really do have loads of money now," I chipped in. "Taking you out is no problem."

"Are you sure?" Laney said doubtfully. "I feel bad not contributing."

"It's all fine!' I declared. "I want you to be able to do lots of stuff with us. Please let us pay."

"All right," she said at last.

After that, the next weeks of the holidays went by in a blur of activity. Laney and I saw a musical and loads of movies, tried ice skating, and took art and craft classes. We even had surfing lessons.

“I love being rich!” I said, as we drove home from the surf park one afternoon in our new family-sized SUV.

Laney smiled. “It is nice,” she said. “But, you know, I still love doing the stuff we’ve always done – like hanging out, doing puzzles, shooting hoops at the park. That’s all good with me.”

I nodded. She was right that the simple things were still nice, but, for me, having all these choices felt truly amazing.

Chapter 2

A New Home

As soon as the lottery money had arrived in Mum and Dad's bank account, Dad quit his job at a car parts warehouse and started house-hunting. He'd soon found a new luxury penthouse apartment for us not too far from where we'd been living.

I could barely believe my eyes when I saw the place. It was massive. There were two huge living areas, heaps of bedrooms and impressive views over the city. The ground floor of the apartment complex also had a gym and a swimming pool, plus a kids' games area with foosball soccer and table tennis.

The first person to visit was Laney. "This is incredible!" she said, as I showed her around.

"I know," I gushed. "I feel like I'm in a movie!"

As well as house-hunting and taking us kids on excursions, Dad had purchased our SUV, organised furniture for our new home – and was taking golf lessons! Along the way, he also discovered a love of shopping.

Every week Dad would buy Freya, Zeb and me gifts. Some, like the purple giraffe hot-water bottle cover and the t-shirt with pictures of bright pink babies, were a bit weird! But in amongst the odd purchases were a few great things. I got an excellent gaming system, and Zeb received the thing he wanted most in the world – a powerful telescope. Luckily our new place was enormous enough to store everything!

Mum, on the other hand, didn't give up work. She just swapped working nights at the hospital for working shorter hours during the day. She told us she liked her job and, with so many big changes, she wanted to keep life as normal as possible – but with some extra family time.

Another part of keeping life normal, Mum told us, was for us kids to continue doing our chores around the house. She put up a new jobs roster for us on the fridge. I was about to start groaning about being overworked when she told me she'd also decided to give us weekly pocket money. I'd never had pocket money before. I felt so grown-up!

Chapter 3

Back to School

A week after we moved, it was time to go back to school. Grade 5! For the past two years, Laney and I had been in the same class, but this year we were separated. I felt nervous because I was going to be in Ms Norris's room with a lot of kids I'd never been with before, including Gwen and Isla.

Gwen and Isla were the coolest girls in our year level. Everyone thought so. They were also the most popular and the most fashionable. Being friends with them made you cool, too. I had never hung out with them, but I knew a bit about them.

I'd heard that Gwen loved shopping and that her family took lots of overseas holidays. I think she liked to ski too. I'd never seen snow.

Isla apparently had a karaoke room and a swimming pool at her house, and everyone said that she had amazing birthday parties! Gwen and Isla always had the coolest and most enviable stuff, like the latest sneakers and those cute rainbow-coloured backpacks we all loved. Everyone wanted to be in their group.

As it turned out, Ms Norris put me on the same table as Gwen. We didn't talk a lot that first day. Gwen was far too busy chatting with her friends at a nearby table. Every now and then I'd glance over at her and think how incredible it must be to be so popular.

It wasn't until after recess on the second day, when Ms Norris announced we were going to work on some maths problems in pairs, that Gwen spoke to me.

"I bet you're good at maths," she said. "Do you want to work together?"

"Sure," I squeaked in surprise, before reaching down to my tub to get some pencils.

When I put my new sequinned pencil case on the table, Gwen let out a gasp. For a moment, I thought something was wrong.

Then she said, "Oh, I love that! It's really pretty."

The sapphire-coloured pencil case was one of Dad's shopping expedition presents. I couldn't believe Gwen was complimenting me about it! Some of the girls at the table behind leant around to look. I heard one of them say, "So cute!"

In just seconds I'd gone from someone who was hardly ever noticed to someone who had something everyone admired. I didn't expect to enjoy being the centre of attention so much. But it felt incredible.

That afternoon, Mum was standing by the school gate. Freya usually walked us home, but today she was waiting alongside Mum as Zeb and I came out of class.

"I got my new zoom-mobile today," Mum said, laughing, as we met up.

I wondered what she was talking about until she pointed to a bright-red sports car parked on the other side of the street. Its new paintwork glinted in the sun.

"Amazing, Mum!" I exclaimed.

"I've always wanted a beautiful car," said Mum. "It's my present to myself."

“Will we all fit in?” I asked, as we walked across the zebra crossing. The back seat looked very small.

“We will if I can get it to open,” said Mum, jabbing at the car key fob in her hand.

Suddenly, a bell-like sound tinged from inside the car as the doors unlocked.

Slinging my bag in the back seat, next to Zeb, I noticed a small group of students near the school gate. Gwen, Isla and some other girls were all staring at us.

It was the second time in one day that I was being noticed by the cool girls.

Feeling suddenly confident, I put my hand up and waved. Gwen grinned and waved back.

Chapter 4

New Friends

At break times, Gwen and her friends always congregated outside at one of the long picnic tables under the trees. As I was walking past at lunchtime the next day, Gwen called me over.

"Sit with us!" she said.

Sit with Gwen and her group? I could hardly believe my ears! But I couldn't join them, because I always had lunch with Laney.

"I'm on my way to meet Laney," I said.

"Just stay for a minute," said Gwen. "Isla's telling us about her birthday party plans."

"Okay," I said, feeling curious and flattered.

Isla was talking about one of her favourite movie characters. "You know that purple sparkly dress she was wearing in the party scene? That's the dress I'm getting made for my party."

"Wow, amazing!" I said. I'd never thought about having a dress specially made before.

Gwen turned to me. "What are you wearing to the party, Willow?"

"Oh," I mumbled. "I haven't been invited."

"You *are* invited!" said Isla. "It's in two weeks. Give me your mum's email address and my mum will send an invitation tonight."

"And Laney?" I asked. "Can she come as well?" I didn't want her to miss out on a party. Besides the fact that we didn't go to many parties, I thought there might be karaoke, and Laney loved karaoke – or at least singing along to the radio.

"Sure," said Isla. "I'll add her too."

I caught up with Laney a few minutes later.

"Guess what!" I said, as we sat down to eat lunch. "We've been invited to Isla's birthday party."

"We have?" said Laney. "Why? How?"

"Isla invited me and I asked if you could come along too. Isn't it exciting?"

"I don't really know her," said Laney, cautiously. "I don't think I'll go."

I kept talking, ignoring what Laney had just said. "I'm going shopping on Saturday for a party dress. Come with me! I can get something for you, too."

Laney frowned. “There’s a basketball pre-season warm-up session,” she said. “Remember?”

“I don’t *have* to go to that, do I?” I asked.

“I guess not,” said Laney quietly.

In class later that day, Gwen mentioned she and Isla were going shopping on Saturday.

“I need a new dress for the party,” she said.

“Me too,” I said.

“Come with us, then,” said Gwen. “It’ll be fun.”

I tried to act as casually as I could. I didn’t want to sound like it was a big thing for me to go shopping with Gwen and Isla. But inside, I could feel my heart beat a little bit faster with excitement. Gwen had invited me shopping! And not only that, I also knew that she and Isla would help me choose exactly the right dress to wear to the party. A dress to impress everyone there.

On Saturday afternoon, Gwen's mum took Isla, Gwen and me to a glitzy mall a few suburbs away. Isla and Gwen led the way to a stylish shop with the best party clothes I had ever seen. Before I knew it, we were flicking through the racks. Isla was having her outfit made, so she didn't need to buy anything – although that didn't stop her trying on a million items. In the end, Gwen selected a lacy white jumpsuit, and I chose a blue satin dress.

Besides dresses, the shop stocked lots of beautiful accessories. All along one counter there were bowls full of rings, bracelets, ribbons and scrunchies. As we browsed, Isla pointed to a pretty necklace in a glass cabinet. "That's adorable!" she said.

A little later, when she went to try on some other clothes, I bought the necklace. It was quite expensive, but now that I had lots of money, buying it was no problem at all. It would be the perfect birthday gift for Isla.

As we wandered off to grab an afternoon snack, I thought briefly about pre-season basketball practice. Maybe I should have gone, but I figured I could catch up on that any time. Meanwhile, I got to hang out with the two coolest girls at school. What could be better than that?

Chapter 5

Party, Party

Isla's party was the following weekend. I had finally convinced Laney it would be good if she came too. But, as we drove to Isla's house with Dad, Laney was strangely quiet. She hadn't even bothered to dress up.

"Aren't you excited about the party?" I said.

"I don't know," she said.

"You'll have fun when we get there," I declared. "The pool will be great."

"Oh," she said. "I didn't bring bathers."

"But I told you we'd swim if it was sunny."

Laney shrugged. "Sorry, I forgot."

When we arrived at the house, the party had already started. Music blared out from the sound system and some kids were dancing in the living room at the back of the house.

Everyone was dressed up, and I fitted in perfectly with my shiny satin dress. People kept telling me how much they loved my outfit. I had never had so many compliments before.

Isla came to greet us. I handed her the present I'd bought at the mall, and when she ripped the wrapping open she let out a squeal. "You knew exactly what I wanted!" she exclaimed in front of about ten other girls. "You are amazing!"

Grinning from the praise, I turned to Laney, but she had gone. Looking around, I saw her making her way out into the back garden.

When I got outside, I found Laney sitting under an umbrella talking to Isla's aunt and nibbling some party snacks. Laney said she'd be fine there while I went for a swim, so I went to get changed.

By the time I jumped in the pool, it was full of kids. Everyone was laughing and shouting, and clambering onto inflatable floating islands. I got carried away playing a ring-toss game and forgot to check on Laney. When I finally turned in her direction, she had disappeared.

Isla's aunt told me Laney's gran had come to get her. *Why had Gran come?* I wondered. I felt worried. I also felt annoyed that Laney hadn't told me she was leaving.

When Mum came for me after the party, she told me Laney's gran had called her about fetching Laney. Apparently, Gran, who lived in the country, had been staying at Laney's. But for some reason, she was returning home early, and Laney was going back with her.

I called Gran on Mum's phone, and Laney answered straightaway.

"Sorry," she said. "I yelled out to you in the pool, but you mustn't have heard. I had to rush because Gran was waiting outside. I'm staying with her tonight."

I wondered if that was an excuse to leave the party early.

"I'll see you on Monday," she blurted, and before I could ask any more, she hung up.

Chapter 6

Different Directions

As it turned out, I didn't see Laney on Monday. After school that afternoon, she rang me and said she was still at her gran's. The phone connection wasn't clear, but I could make out words like "Gran" and "not well" and "Mum and I ... staying here for a few days."

Luckily, I now had Gwen and Isla's group to spend break times at school with. So, I joined them every recess and lunchtime while Laney was away. I mostly listened while they discussed fashion and celebrity gossip. It was so different from spending time with Laney. But still, I didn't mind. All the things they were interested in were cool. Everyone said so.

When Laney returned to school the following week, I asked her to join the group at break times too, but she shook her head.

"I'm practising for the basketball season," she said. "I want to get into the senior team."

The senior team was the top basketball team at school. It was mostly full of grade sixes, but a few good grade five players were often included.

"Don't you want to be part of that team, too?" she said.

I shrugged. "I like hanging out with the other girls. It's fun to be in their group."

Laney gave me a slightly doubtful look. "Okay," she said. "It's your choice."

The weeks went by, and I hardly noticed that I was seeing less and less of Laney. We still met up at pre-season basketball training once a week, but she didn't come to my place nearly as often. Instead, I was spending more time with Gwen and Isla. I'd ask Laney along on these excursions too, but even when I said I could pay for her, she always had an excuse. She'd say that she needed to do something for her mum, or she was going to her gran's or practising for basketball.

I started to invite Gwen and Isla and some of their other friends to come over after school. Dad had a new favourite activity – cooking. He was doing a pastry-making course, and he was really good at it. He made us the most amazing afternoon teas. Everyone loved his chocolate biscuits, cheese twists and almond croissants, which we would scoff down while watching movies or fashion shows online.

I also made sure there was something for everyone to take home each time they visited, like a bright-coloured nail polish, a cute notebook or a little pot of lip balm. I wanted the girls to love coming to my place and to always want to return.

Towards the end of term, Ms Raymond, our PE teacher and basketball coach, announced the school's senior representative basketball players at assembly. When she read out Laney's name, I've never seen anyone so happy. Laney couldn't stop jumping up and down for ages.

"You should be in the senior team, too," she said to me, as we talked near the lockers later. "You're such a good player. We've both wanted to do this since grade three. What happened?"

"I guess I'm not so interested anymore," I said, shrugging. "Maybe I'll play in it next year."

"You won't if you keep hanging out with Isla and Gwen," she countered. "They're not interested in basketball."

“Basketball isn’t everything,” I said, feeling defensive now. “I’m doing all sorts of other things with them. We have a great time. You should join us sometimes. And you don’t have to worry if you can’t afford things. I can pay for you.”

Laney looked angry then. “I don’t want you to pay for me,” she snapped. “I just want us to hang out and do the stuff we used to do. That was fun. But you don’t seem to care about that kind of fun now. You just want to be cool.”

I opened my mouth to reply, but Laney walked away before I could work out what to say.

The school holidays started the following week. Mum and Dad had planned a break for us, and we spent five days away, visiting theme and water parks. Freya and Zeb each brought a friend, but I hadn't invited anyone.

I found myself missing Laney. I kept thinking about her and wondering what she was up to. I used Mum's phone to message Laney's mum's phone.

It wasn't until we were about to fly home that Laney finally messaged back. She said she was at her gran's again and would be there for the rest of the holidays.

"See you next week at school," she wrote, adding a smiley face. That was good. At least she wasn't still cross with me.

When we were back at home, Isla invited me and a couple of other girls to her place one day for a karaoke session. After we'd finished singing, none of us was quite sure what to do next.

"Perhaps we could play a board game," I ventured.

Isla gave me a cool look. "Board games make me bored," she said, putting her hand over her mouth and fake yawning.

"Oh, you're so funny, Isla," said one of the others.

Is she funny? I pondered. I'd never laughed much with Isla. Or even with Gwen. I realised the only friend I really laughed a lot with was Laney. Sometimes we laughed until we cried.

Chapter 7

A Change of Plan

It was before class on the first day of the new term when Ms Raymond approached me.

"I was wondering if you want to come and practise with the senior team later this week," she said.

"The senior team?" I repeated, not sure if I had heard her properly.

"That's right," said Ms Raymond. "We have an unusual situation with several members being sick or away for extended periods. I want to make sure there will be enough players, just in case. So, I thought I would add you to our numbers."

I felt slightly shocked. "I didn't think I was good enough," I blurted.

“You have great potential, Willow,” she said. “You just need to put more time in. Are you willing to do that?”

A strange sense of excitement rushed through me. “I am!” I replied, realising how much it meant to be chosen for that team.

“Fantastic!” said Ms Raymond.

When I went into class, I couldn’t wait to tell Gwen and Isla the incredible news about getting into the team.

“That’s great,” said Gwen.

“What a star,” said Isla.

But despite their kind words, I knew they weren’t really interested. This was something only Laney would get. Actually, she was the only person I really wanted to tell. But she was one of the players who was away – one that I might be replacing. It just didn’t seem right, or very fair.

When I got home from school, I told Mum what Ms Raymond had said.

"That's fantastic about getting into the team!" she said. Then she looked at me with what I call her serious face.

"But the news about Laney doesn't sound so good. Her gran must be quite ill."

"I don't know," I said. "She didn't come to school again today."

Mum frowned. "You and Laney don't seem to be seeing much of each other at the moment," she said.

"We're doing different things right now," I replied, hoping Mum wasn't going to ask me more. I wanted to message Laney to ask why she wasn't at school again, but I didn't know what to say. It had never been difficult to talk to her before.

I was relieved when Mum said, “Well, I’ll give Laney’s mum a ring later and see if they are all right.”

Later, Mum told me that she’d tried to get hold of Laney’s mum several times but that she hadn’t been answering her phone.

“I hope everything is okay,” she said, looking concerned.

“Me too,” I said.

Laney and I hadn’t been in touch since the last week of the holidays, so I hadn’t known she was still away. Once, I would have known about everything that happened in her life, but now, I hardly had any idea.

Chapter 8

Helping Out

Laney came back to school a couple of days later. I saw her walking across the playground at recess, and I ran over to her. I was fairly sure her last message meant she wasn't still mad with me.

"Is everything okay? I asked. "You've been away so much. Is your gran all right?"

When she turned to me I noticed she looked pale and tired. She also looked a little confused. "Gran is fine," she said. "It's Mum who has been ill."

"Oh," I said, realising I'd mixed up the facts. "Is your mum okay now?"

Laney took a deep breath. "Mum came out of hospital on the weekend, which is great. And Gran says Mum's 'on the mend' now, but I don't know. The doctors said she'll have to go back for more treatment at some point."

"Do you need anything?" I asked.

"No, no," she replied quickly. "We'll be fine. It'll all be fine. Don't worry."

But I was worried. After all, she was my oldest and best friend.

When I got home from school that afternoon, Mum told me that Laney's gran had rung her.

"She explained all about Laney's mum being ill and that she's been in and out of hospital for tests and treatment for a while now," she said.

"Is there a way we can help them?" I asked.

Mum smiled. "I think there might be."

The next day, Mum came to pick me up from school. Zeb was going to play with a friend, so it was just us. We were going to give Laney a lift back to her place. We waited at the front gate until she appeared.

"Want a ride in my zoom-mobile?" Mum said to Laney.

Laney looked at me and we both giggled. "I would love to," she said.

At Laney's house, our mothers had a long chat in the living room, while Laney and I played a board game at the kitchen table.

"I've missed doing this," I said.

"Me too," said Laney.

After a while, Mum called us to join them.

"Laney, would you like to stay with us when your mum goes back to hospital?" Mum asked.

"Gran lives so far away from here and school," added Laney's mum. "So, it would be great for you to stay nearby. And with friends. Of course, if you don't want to, you don't have to."

I don't think I'd ever seen Laney cry before, except when she came off her bike and badly gashed her knee in grade four. Now, her eyes brimmed with tears.

"Thank you!" she said, looking from me to Mum. "I would love to stay with you!"

Chapter 9

What Really Matters

Laney moved into our spare room a few weeks later and stayed with us for a month while her mum was in hospital and recovering. We spent a lot of time together and when we weren't practising or playing basketball, we were playing board games, hanging out in the recreation area downstairs, and laughing at the silliest things possible.

One night at dinner, Dad announced he was going to study business management. This would give him the skills for him and Mum to set up a medical research charity to help people like Laney's mum.

"I think it takes a while to get used to being suddenly rich," Dad said thoughtfully. "Mum and I have been thinking a lot about what to do with our money. Helping Laney and her mum made us realise how much we could do for others."

After dinner, Laney and I went downstairs to play table tennis.

"I'm so glad you came to stay," I said, as we got into the lift. "I'm sorry that I wasn't a good friend last term. Being suddenly rich went to my head! I got caught up in being popular and forgot about things that really matter – like good friendships. Money can never buy those."

"It can't," said Laney. "But you know, your money has helped us a lot too. I've been able to stay here, and you've paid for extra help at home for Mum. So, thank you!"

"My pleasure; our pleasure," I said with a bow, and then we high fived.

I'm still friendly with Gwen and Isla and their group. We spend time together in class and even occasionally at break times, too. I invited them all to my birthday party recently. We had karaoke in the games room downstairs, and Dad made a huge choc-caramel birthday cake, which everyone loved. I got lots of presents. Surprisingly, one of the best ones was from Isla. It was a super pack of the "World's Best Board Games".